The kookie cooks at MAD have mixed up this latest potpourri of lip-smacking lunacy . . . flavored it with spicy satires, peppery parodies and saucy spoofs . . . and topped it all off with the "Ac'cent" on laughs.

We're ready to serve you heaping portions of "Minced Madison Avenue," "Ground-up Hollywood," "Creamed TV" and "Chopped Politics" . . . and we're sure you'll savor every bite we take out of these half-baked Sacred Cows.

So get ready to dig in to a feast fit for a king-size clod. Fork over our $1.25 cover charge to that hungry Book Dealer who's dying to wait on you . . . dip into this mouth-watering assortment of goodies . . . and digest

BOILING MAD

You'll enjoy it . . . if you can stomach it!

William M. Gaines's
Boiling°

Editor
Albert B. Feldstein

WARNER BOOKS

A Warner Communications Company

Warner Books, Inc.
666 Fifth Avenue
New York, N.Y. 10103

 A Warner Communications Company

Printed in the United States of America

First Printing: December, 1973

Reissued: November, 1986

10 9 8

CONTENTS

There are handy phrase books available to Americans traveling to Iceland, Greenland, Poland, etc., which help them to understand the foreign languages spoken in these countries. However, there are no handy phrase books available to Americans remaining at home which help them to understand some of the foreign languages spoken right here in the good ol' U.S.A. . . . in places like Wall Street, Madison Avenue and Televisionland. And so, in order to fill this great need, the Editors present

MAD'S HANDY GUIDE TO LANGUAGES OF THE U.S.A.

"This is a very thorough presentation, Sudbury, and I want you to know that I appreciate the work you've put into finalizing it!"	"If I have anythin to say about it, yo will never get out the Mail Room!"
"Just talking off the top of my head, I would say it looks pretty good!"	"I've been trying think of the same thing all week!"
"Of course, you realize that the advertising and promotion of automobile crankshafts is still a relatively new area for exploration and exploitation, and being of such a complicated and diverse nature, I'll have to give this prospectus some long, careful, deliberate, and thoughtful consideration before arriving at a conclusion as to its ultimate merits!"	"I don't make any the decisions aro⋅ here!"
"If it looks like it has what it takes, I'll send it over to the 'Consumer Research, Reaction, and Usage' boys for a test-run examination and analysis, motivational-wise and psychological-wise!"	"I'll send it over to my Brother-in-and he'll try to guess whether or it will work!"

8

"If they like it, I'll take it back under advisement, and give it my personal attention — expanding — polishing, fertilizing and developing!"

"I'll copy the whole thing over in my own handwriting!"

"You may not recognize the end-product . . ."

"And then I'll put my name on it!"

"But don't let that discourage you. Anytime you get another germ of an idea, remember that the door to my office is always open!"

"If I steal six more ideas like this by December, I get a Christmas bonus!"

"Looking for a good used car, eh? Well, I've got a real honey that just came on the lot!"	"Looking for trouble, eh? Well, I've got a real lemon here that I've been trying to get rid of for six months!"
"This baby will give you years of trouble-free transportation!"	"However, I'll only guarantee it for 30 days, except parts and labor!"
"It's a one-owner car—"	"The Acme Finance Company!"
"With low mileage on it!"	"The speedometer's busted . . ."
"And it's never been driven over 50 miles an hour . . ."	"Because it won't go any faster . . ."
"It's a good clean car!"	"We just washed it!"
"And it's spotless inside!"	"We forgot to roll up the windows during last night's rainstorm!"
"A two-toned beauty!"	"Half the paint is faded!"
"Starts up almost instantly!"	"The battery's been on charge all day!"

SALESMEN

"I have the garage service records, and I can show you this car has never had to be repaired!"	"It's ready to start wearing out the minute you drive it off the lot!"
"And don't worry about money! We use Bank Financing!"	"We borrow the money from a bank at 5% and charge you 12%!"

"You can rely on us because we depend on repeat customers to stay in business!"	"Anybody idiotic enough to buy a car from us is idiotic enough to come back again!"

"Ladies and Gentlemen, I invited you all to gather here this afternoon to introduce you to Mr. Herkimer Asmuth!"

"By 'invited,' I mean there will be no overtime pay for the night shift, even though the had to get out of bed to attend this meeting

"Mr. Asmuth is part of this company's long range executive expansion program ..."

"Another one of my daughters got marrie By 'long range,' I mean I still got two daughters to go!"

EXECUTIVES

"... and he will assume the position of 'Executive Staff Personnel Advisor to the President's Office'!"	"It doesn't sound so much like feather-bedding if the title is big enough!"
"He comes to us direct from Baldwin & Benedict University, where he was tops in his class!"	"As a Major in Greek Mythology!"
"I feel that this bright young executive has a real future with our company!"	"Naturally, if they invent a machine to replace him, we won't buy it!"
"I am confident that everyone here will pitch in and help Mr. Asmuth learn the ropes!"	"For heaven's sake, keep an eye on him so he doesn't make some fool mistake that would put us out of business!"
"So, let's all make him feel welcome!"	"No funny pictures on the Bulletin Board, or obscene comments in the Suggestion Box, please!"
"That's all I have to say at this time!"	"Your lunch hour is over, so back to work!"

INTERPRETING THE LANGUAGE OF
UNIONS

"Because the cost of living has gone up faster than the Company's wages, many of the Union members are going broke!"	"The Union raised its dues again, and some of its members can't afford to pay them, so we want our demands met this time"
"Our ultimate and final demand is a 25¢ an hour pay increase!"	"We will accept a 5¢ an hour raise!"
"We demand 4 weeks vacation with pay; two weeks in the Summer and two weeks in the Winter, plus all Holidays including St. Patrick's Day and Halloween, with each worker getting his birthday off!"	"As far as vacations and time off go, things are all right the way they are: Two weeks with pay, and Holidays!"
"We demand a 30-hour work week, consisting of 5 six-hour days, or 4 seven-and-a-half hour days!"	"We really think this demand is ridiculous, but our membership will love us for asking!"
"We propose that, for the good of the Company, all overtime be eliminated in favor of hiring more manpower!"	"We don't care if you hire anybody else or not, as long as you don't fire anybody!"

AUCTIO

"Because of the Union's absurd demands during the last contract negotiations, the Company is now going broke!"	"The Company's profits are down to $9,000,000, so we want our demands met this time!"
"Our ultimate and final offer is to cut wages 25¢ an hour!"	"A 5¢ an hour raise is as high as we will go!"
"We refuse to offer anything more than one week vacation without pay, and Easter Sunday off!"	"As far as vacations and time off go, things are all right the way they are: Two weeks with pay, and Holidays!"
We demand a 55 hour workweek, consisting of 7 eight hour days with one hour off on Sundays for church!"	"We really think this demand is ridiculous, but our stockholders will love us for asking!"
"We have always been a friend of Labor, and will certainly consider hiring as many men as possible!"	"If there is some way of doing without any of you, we would! Rest assured we're looking into Automation!"

"The program originally scheduled for this time will not be seen . . ."	"Some idiot in Master Control accidentally erased the tape!"
"The following program is brought to you in Living Color . . ."	"We've been presenting color programs for five years now! When the hell are you people out there going to start buying color TV sets?"
"Tonight's show is brought to you spontaneous and unrehearsed!"	"Nobody showed up for rehearsal, so we're going to read the whole thing off the Teleprompter!"
"America's newest television game . . ."	"Quiz Shows are back!"
"Here to try for the $500 jackpot . . ."	"Only the prizes ain't what they used to be since the investigations!"
"And now, before I introduce . . ."	"Here's the first commercial . . ."
"Our group had 47% fewer cavities . . ."	"Mainly because we've got 57% fewer teeth!"
"Our first guest has a very unusual voice . . ."	"This girl can't sing!"

TELEVISION

"She's one of America's great song stylists . . ."

"So she covers up her lack of talent by screaming!"

| "I'm sure you'll enjoy listening to her . . ." | "Because she's funnier than our comedian!" |
| "And now, here's a word from our alternate sponsor . . ." | "Bet you didn't think we had the nerve to throw in another commercial!" |

18

"It's just like a Doctor's prescription..."	"Overpriced!"
"Our next guest is a different kind of comedian..."	"He doesn't get any laughs!"
"You'll be hearing a lot about him in the next few months..."	"He's running around with a married woman!"
"And now...a short pause for station identification..."	"Which includes a one-minute commercial, a 30-second network promotion, a 10-second spot ad, and another one-minute commercial—so here's your chance to grab a snack!"
"Come in, 'Mystery Guest' – and sign in, please!"	"Come in, whichever movie star happens to be in town tonight, and plug your latest picture..."
"The following program is brought to you as a Public Service..."	"Our Sales Department couldn't line up a sponsor for this bomb!"
"This station is a subscriber to the Television Code..."	"It makes for interesting reading, even though we ignore it!"

Don Martin, MAD's maddest artist, is "disturbed" by many things, one being modern transportation which he claims aggravates his "split personality". For example, observe what happened to Don the day he tried to keep

THE
APPOINTMENT

I

4

22

O.MARTIN

MAD dedicates this next article to all those who have ever been nauseated by stale jokes, soggy hors d'oeuvres, warm beer, cold stares, dry conversation, wet blankets, loose gossip, and tight guests (both invited and uninvited)! In other words, let's take a quick look at—

the lighter side
of
ENTERTAINING

Good Heavens !!...
Charlie and Claire
Dellune just drove up!!

29

37

You MAD readers who, through some extraordinary combination of luck and circumstance, found yourselves newly arrived on college campuses this year, may now be wondering whether or not to join a fraternity—in the unlikely event that you might be asked. During the "Rushing Season," suave frat men will woo you with extravagant sales pitches for their organizations—and since most of you are undoubtedly naive and inexperienced clods, you may be completely snowed under by this deluge of propaganda. To educate you, and at the same time protect you, MAD now turns a very skeptical eye on the claims that are made by . . .

WHAT THEY SAY...

"You'll live in a beautiful, impressive house!"

"Your frat brothers will be a swell bunch of guys!"

College Fraternities

WHAT WE SAY...

Make sure you come back and inspect the premises carefully in broad daylight!

Be sure you meet *all* the members. They usually hide the clods and creeps until after Rushing Season!

"You'll eat delicious home-cooked meals!"

"You'll enjoy attractive, comfortable living quarters!"

Get a peek at the kitchen and the cook—because
they probably *sent out* for the meal they gave you!

Only you won't be sleeping in the living room,
so you'd better take a look upstairs! (*Eccchh!*)

"Upperclass brothers will help with your homework!"

"You'll participate in extracurricular activities!"

—By making it impossible to do it—or get any
studying done unless you flee to the library!

—At your own risk, of course!

"You'll learn about good citizenship
by working on various civic projects!"

"You'll have a great time at all the terrific parties!"

And you'll learn about jails—if you're caught!

—If your idea of having a great time is
watching a lot of other guys throw up!

49

"The small cost of your fraternity membership
will prove to be a profitable investment!"

"You'll join in the crazy stunts, humorous gags,
and general fun when new members are initiated!"

—Profitable is right! For the fraternity treasury!

During wartime, "stunts" and "gags"
like these are known as "Atrocities"!

"Frats judge prospective members by their CHARACTER!"

CHECK LIST FOR
PROSPECTIVE MEMBERS

C AR ☑

H AIRCUT ☐

A NCESTRY ☐

R ELIGION ☐

A LLOWANCE ☐

C ONNECTIONS ☐

T AILORING ☐

E MPLOYMENT (of Father) ☐

R ESIDENCE (of Family) ☐

Scenes

We'd Like to See

The Abominable Snowman

SCREW-BALL IN THE BACK POCKET DEPT.

Once again, MAD presents the feature based on the proposition that you can tell an awful lot about a person when you study the contents of his wallet—like f'rinstance how good his lawyers are when they sue you for publishing personal stuff. Anyway, here's our *fictionalized version* of things we would *probably* find if we were to examine the contents of

CELEBRITIES

WALLETS

NAME: *Jerry Lewis*

ADDRESS: *Hollywood Calif. & Newark N.J.*

OCCUPATION *Actor, Producer, Director, Singer, Comedian, Composer, Master of Ceremonies, Pantomimist, Orchestra Leader, Musical Arranger, Tap Dancer, Ballet Dancer, Dancer of Kazatsky at Weddings & Bar Mitzvahs, Recording Star, TV Producer, Talent Scout, Business Man, Author, Fund Raiser for Charities, Philosopher, Martyr, (continued on other side of card)*

1962 AWARDS COMMITTEE

THE MOTION PICTURE ACADEMY
OF ARTS AND SCIENCES

Hollywood Boulevard, Hollywood, Calif.

Dear Mr. Lewis:-

Thank you for once again volunteering for the "Academy Awards Show". We might be able to use you. However, we <u>do</u> feel that you are asking a little <u>too much</u> when you demand to be the Master of Ceremonies--<u>and</u> sing the five Nominated Songs--<u>and</u> open all the Envelopes while making funny faces.

Very truly yours,

Eugene Klotzberg

Eugene Klotzberg,
Chairman

SATURDAY
OCTOBER 15, 1949

THINGS TO DO TODAY

Ride downtown in a taxi while standing up through the "Sky View", hollering.

Butter somebody's necktie.

Doodle on somebody's shirtsleeve.

Nail somebody's shoes to the floor.

Cut somebody's suspenders with a scissor.

Drop bags of water out dressing room window.

Finster, Hagen and Schnook

ATTORNEYS-AT-LAW
HOLLYWOOD, CALIFORNIA

Dear Mr. Lewis:-

We realize that you have suffered
a certain amount of hardship and
financial reverses as a result of
the break-up between you and our
client, Mr. Dean Martin. However,
we feel that your request is a bit
unusual, and absolutely out of the
question!

There is really <u>no legal reason</u> why
he should pay you <u>"Alimony"</u>!

Sincerely yours,

Irving Finster

Irving Finster

SATURDAY
JANUARY 27, 1962

<u>THINGS TO DO TODAY !</u>

Show orchestra how to run through
    Gershwin number.

Fire script girl who coughed during
    my Pantomime scene yesterday.

Order #400. "Director's Chair" from N.Y.

Lunch with David Susskind

Order 14 new chamois-lined suits
    from Don Loper.

Help out Kazan with his 2nd scene

59

VARIETY

CLASSIFIED AD DEPT.

TO: Mr. Jerry Lewis #7838652

PLEASE REMIT $280.00

In payment for following ad, which has appeared every issue since November 8 as per your instructions, and will continue to run until we are notified otherwise. Please check if copy meets your specifications.

WANTED

TALL, GOOD-LOOKING SINGER who can take orders, to team up with established comedian as straight man. Immediate position available. Reply Box 79, Hollywood.

PROOF

Local 137

Restaurant Workers of America

Hollywood, Calif.

Dear Mr. Lewis:-

Thank you for your informative letter. We were not aware that the help at "Dino's Restaurant", owned by a Mr. D. Martin, was non-union. We will of course set up picket lines immediately. You have done your duty as an American, a friend of Labor, and a member of your community.

Very truly yours,

Kenneth Rapieff

Kenneth Rapieff
33rd Vice President

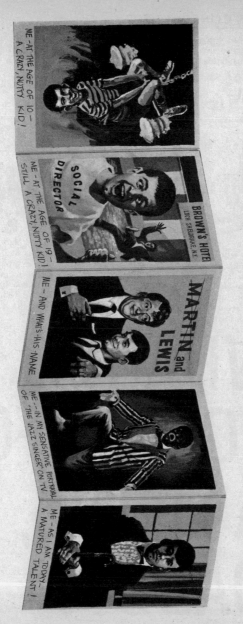

ME – AT THE AGE OF 10 – A CRAZY, NUTTY KID !

SOCIAL DIRECTOR

BROWN'S HOTEL
LOCH SHELDRAKE, N.Y.

ME – AT THE AGE OF 19 – STILL A CRAZY, NUTTY KID !

MARTIN and LEWIS

ME – AND WHAT'S-HIS-NAME

ME – IN MY SENSATIVE PORTRAYAL OF "THE JAZZ SINGER" ON TV

ME – AS I AM TODAY – A MATURED TALENT !

There will come a time in the life of every father when his little son or daughter will suddenly ask, "What do you do for a living, Daddy?" For most fathers, this question poses no great problem. They will merely say . . .

Daddy is a salesman, dear! He sells shoes!

or . . .

Daddy is a cop, son! He arrests bad men!

or . . .

Daddy is a crook, child! He publishes MAD Magazine!

However, in the high-powered age we live in today, there are many fathers who make their livings in complicated ways (called "rackets") as trained experts (called "phony experts"). These guys are really stuck when it comes to explaining to their innocent offspring how they make a buck. The child, being young and naive, tends to see things in basic, simple, and unsophisticated terms. Take the following cases of fathers with complicated occupations. Here's what can happen when their kids ask . . .

WHAT DO YOU DO FOR A LIVING, DADDY?

A PSYCHIATRIST

65

**DOMESTIC RELATIONS
COUNSELOR**

PUBLIC RELATIONS MAN

73

What do you do for a living, Daddy?

CHILD GUIDANCE CONSULTANT

Daddy is a "Child Guidance Consultant," dear. Parents engage me to throw light on their child-rearing problems!

Here's MAD'S maddest artist, Don Martin, and his tongue-depressor-in-cheek version of what happened when he was—

IN A DOCTOR'S OFFICE

Dentists are really happy guys, even if they're always looking "down in the mouth"—not because they're filling an emptiness in your life, but because you're filling an emptiness in theirs —mainly in their wallets! And so, with "tongue-in-cheek" (where he may not be able to reach it with his drill), MAD now grinds out a look at—

the
lighter
side of the
DENTIST

CONTINUED ON PAGE 78

This child has an abnormal amount of cavities!!

She gets them from eating too much candy! The sugar eats holes in the enamel, encouraging decay! The trouble with you parents today is: Instead of good old fashioned discipline you use **candy as bribery**!!

Sit still, sweetheart Musn't bite the dentist, dear! Don't play with the water!! Le'go of the drill!!

If you're a good girl, and let me do my work . . . when I'm through, I'll give you a **lollypop**!!

94   END

When Fidel (the man with the sword) ordered Antonio Prohias (the man with the pen) arrested for his anti-Castro cartoons, the Cuban artist fled to the U.S., where he now graces MAD's pages with...

In 1897, Marconi invented the first wireless radio, which enabled man to transmit his voice across space . . . while Sidney L. Kvetch was clearing his snow-covered walk with a shovel.

In 1923, V. K. Zworykin invented the image iconoscope, which enabled man to transmit pictures across space — while Sidney L. Kvetch Jr. cleared his snow-covered walk with a shovel.

MORE
SNOW

HEAVY SNOWFALLS
PARALYZE MODERN LIFE

TYPICAL LITTLE TOWN PARALYZED BY SNOW: Although this typical little town looks picturesque and peaceful under its blanket of snow, it is actually in terrible shape . . . mainly because this typical little town is New York City!

In 1961, Wernher Von Braun developed a missile program which enabled man to transmit himself across space—while Sidney L. Kvetch III cleared his snow-covered walk with a shovel.

THIS IS KNOWN AS PROGRESS!

EFFICIENT REMOVAL

HOW HEAVY SNOWS PARALYZE

PARALYZED TRAFFIC

City traffic, locked in by snow, cannot budge. Of course, it cannot budge in summer either, but at least there are pretty girls in clinging dresses to watch while waiting.

PARALYZED CONSUMER TRADE

Naturally, retail businessmen suffer acutely during snow, except for a few opportunists who do well. Paralysis sets in when consumer hears prices of needed shovel, salt, etc.

MODERN LIFE IN THE CITY

PARALYZED COMMUTERS

Commuters in stalled trains are in real trouble. Hunger, coughing, tardiness are annoying. But real trouble comes from paralysis which sets in when heating systems fail.

PARALYZED PEDESTRIANS

Frigid weather accompanying snow forces many pedestrians to seek shelter and warming drink. Paralysis sets in when too many warming drinks turn pedestrians stiff as boards.

MECHANICAL SNOW MELTING PROCESS

**This suggested solution involves a special machine wh
is mounted on a truck and shoots a jet stream of hot**

**Unfortunately, there are several drawbacks to this id
First of all, if the jet stream of air is hot enough,**

at the snow. Of course, this jet stream must be quite hot, otherwise winter temperatures would render it ineffective.

melts more than just the snow. Secondly, the melted snow soon freezes over again, locking everything in solid ice.

CHEMICAL SNOW MELTING PROCESS

This ingenious solution requires the use of helicopter
which sprinkle the city with thousands of gallons of som

Unfortunately, it does not solve the water problem, since
there is no sewer system yet devised capable of handling

...ecially-developed chemical that melts snow and does not ...mit it to freeze again. This solves the snow problem.

...much melted snow at one time. Obviously, the present ...tions to the problem of snow removal are inadequate.

MAD'S ULTIMATE SOLUTION TO THE PROBLEM OF SNOW REMOVAL

THIS BRILLIANT IDEA IS OFFERED BY THE EDITORS—FREE—AS A PUBLIC SERVI

When Weather Bureau predicts imminent snowstorm, police, civil defense co
etc., see to it that all city streets and sidewalks are immediately evacua

Thousands of dump trucks, previously chartered for just such an emergency,
then driven in and parked on every square inch of city streets and sidewal

When blizzard strikes and snow begins falling, it merely fills up the tru
Then, after the storm passes, all they do is drive away and dump their lo

106   END

CHAPTER I

SPITTIN' ON THE IMAGE DEPT.

Every day, millions of Americans are forced to make important decisions—decisions that affect their very lives—namely: which TV shows to watch! And so, every day, millions of Americans turn to newspapers and TV Guide-type magazines for assistance in making these decisions. And they make these decisions based on the "Capsuled Descriptions" of the shows these publications carry. Which is all very well, except that these "Capsuled Descriptions" are not very accurate. What they describe you do not see! In fact, television fare could be a lot more fun and entertainment . . .

IF TV SHOWS WERE ACTUALLY LIKE THEIR "CAPSULED DESCRIPTIONS"

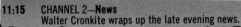

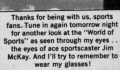

109

10:00   CHANNEL 11—**Bold Journey**
   Tonight, Dr. Leonard Seewald shows us some film he shot while visiting
   the savage Headshrinkers of the Upper Amazon. Jack Douglas is host.

Welcome to "Bold Journey"! I am your host, Jack Douglas—and tonight we're going to meet Dr. Leonard Seewald who will show us some film he shot while visiting the savage Headshrinkers of the Upper Amazon.

Welcome to "Bold Journey", Dr. Seewald!

Thank you, Mr. Douglas . . . and here is the film I shot while visiting the savage Headshrinkers of the Upper Amazon . . .

Notice all them little holes? You see, the film was in my knapsack when my gun went off accidently . . .

Thank you, Dr. Seewald. Folks, be sure and join us again next week when Dr. Seewald will show us some color slides he also shot while visiting the savage Headshrinkers of the Upper Amazon! Goodnight . . .

9:00   CHANNEL 5—**Championship Wrestling**
Chicken Charlie meets Nick The Greek and the Masked Bone Crusher
meets Killer Kowalski at St. Nicholas Arena.

111

The other day in a supermarket, we picked up something called a "TV Dinner"—but the manager was watching so we hadda put it back. Anyway, it got us thinking. Since "TV Dinners" are frozen meals arranged on a tray that the housewife simply heats and has to serve her family while they're huddled around the television set, it seems to us that the manufacturers are missing a good bet. Mainly, why not offer the public—

TV DINNERS

TO MATCH THE SHOWS

or PRIVATE EYE Shows

. . . HARD BOILED EGGS
. . . HOT TOMATOES
. . . Assorted CAPERS

For SITUATION COMEDIES

. . . CORN on the COB
. . . Stale Old CHESTNUTS
. . . Canned YAK

For WRESTLING MATCHES

... Half-Baked HAMS
... SQUASH
... RASPBERRIES

For BOXING MATCHES

... PIGS KNUCK
... BLACK EYE
... MINCEMEAT

For BASEBALL GAMES

... HOT BEEF
... Strained RHUBARB
... GOOSE EGGS

For CONGRESSIONAL HEARIN

... RED HERR
... Hot POTAT
... Cooked GO

For MONSTER MOVIES

... BLOOD SAUSAGE
... LADY FINGERS
... Assorted NUTS

For NEWSCASTS

... Hot LEEK with RELIABLE SAUCE
... Fresh BEETS
... Cream of MUSH

—And For Those COMMERCIALS

... Thinly-Sliced BOLOGNA
... Marinated TRIPE
... PURE APPLESAUCE

END   117

A harried housewife takes pen-in-dish-pan-hand to express her jealousy, fear, and anger at what she considers a threat to her home and marriage:

THE INFERNAL TRIANGLE

(TELEVISION-WISE)

by Lois Carpenter

The "Other Woman" in my life
   Is television's "Perfect Wife"
From breakfast, when her children rush
   Off, saying they've no time to brush,
To afternoon, when in they breeze
   With shouts of "Look, no cavities!"
She spends her time advising me
   That I, too, can live graciously.
She paints her whole house in one day,

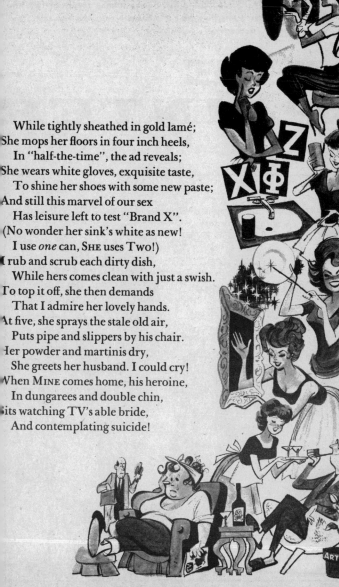

While tightly sheathed in gold lamé;
She mops her floors in four inch heels,
  In "half-the-time", the ad reveals;
She wears white gloves, exquisite taste,
  To shine her shoes with some new paste;
And still this marvel of our sex
  Has leisure left to test "Brand X".
(No wonder her sink's white as new!
  I use *one* can, SHE uses Two!)
I rub and scrub each dirty dish,
  While hers comes clean with just a swish.
To top it off, she then demands
  That I admire her lovely hands.
At five, she sprays the stale old air,
  Puts pipe and slippers by his chair.
Her powder and martinis dry,
  She greets her husband. I could cry!
When MINE comes home, his heroine,
  In dungarees and double chin,
Sits watching TV's able bride,
  And contemplating suicide!

END   119

Don Martin, MAD'S maddest artist, comes from a family of folk who draw. His brother draws flies, his sister draws blood, and his uncle draws unemployment insurance as . . .

THE
PAINTER

SISS-BOOM-BLAH DEPT.

Almost every large school today concentrates on major sports like basketball, football and baseball. These schools have lots of money for the best coaches and players available. But what about the little school that can't come up with the scratch to field a basketball, football or baseball team? What can they do? We'll tell you what they can do! They can concentrate on minor inexpensive sports like ping-pong, bowling and bridge! And the students can show their support singing these . . .

Fight Songs For

Schools That Can't Afford Major Sports

— for Wrestling Squads

ON YOU KIDNEY CRUNCHERS
(to the tune of "The Song of the Vagabonds")

On you kidney crunchers!
On you rabbit punchers!
Grunt! Grunt! Grunt to victory!
Twist them into jelly!
Stomp upon their belly!
Grunt! Grunt! Grunt to victory!
Crush their necks until they gasp for air!
Gouge their eyes and pull them by the hair!
Smash an organ vital!
And you'll win the title!
Grunt! Grunt! Grunt to victory!

— for Bowling Teams

ROLL THE BALL
(to the tune of "Over There")

Roll the ball!
Roll the ball!
We can win! Groove it in! Roll the ball!
It's a crucial frame, now,
So take good aim, now,
And you will see the pins all fall!
Do not stall!
Get 'em all!
Make 'em crash with a smash 'gainst the wall!
We're in clover!
You knocked 'em over!
And we would have won if you'd let go of the ball!

— for Chess Squads

BISHOPS AWAY
(to the tune of "Anchors Aweigh")

Bishops away, my lads!
Bishops away!
Move up those knights and pawns
And keep your queen in play-ay-ay-ay!
Castle your king, my lads!
Don't hesitate!
Whoops! Guess we told you wrong!
He's got you there!
He's got you there!
Check-Mate!

CHEER, CHEER FOR OUR SCRABBLE SQUAD
(to the tune of "Cheer, Cheer for Old Notre Dame")

Cheer, cheer for our Scrabble squad!
They fill the board with words that are odd!
ADZ and XEBEC, ZAX and QUA,
ZARF and QUINOA, PYX and KA!
JATO and FURZY; OS, UT and UGH,
ZYGOTE and BABA, YOHO and VUG!
They know every word except
The one that spells VICTORY!

— for Monopoly Teams

FROM THE SLUMS OF BALTIC AVENUE
(to the tune of "From the Halls of Montezuma")

From the slums of Baltic Av-e-nue
'Round to Boardwalk and Park Place —
We will buy up all the prop-er-ties,
Build hotels on every space!
We will drive our foes to bank-rupt-cy
If they fail to pay the price!
But we cannot even start the game
Till somebody finds the dice!

129

— for Crap-Shooting Teams

ON YOU SHOOTERS
(to the tune of "On Wisconsin")

On you shooters!
On you shooters!
Get down on your knees!
Roll a seven! Roll eleven!
Don't make boxcars, please (or snake-eyes)!
Show your class, boys!
Make that pass, boys!
Then you'll hear us shout!
And our cheering will not stop
Till you crap out!

THE BRIDGE TEAM GOES RUFFING ALONG
(to the tune of "The Caissons Go Rolling Along")

Bid a heart!
Bid a spade!
Bid a game that can't be made!
As the Bridge Team goes ruffing along!
Lose a slam
By a trick!
See your partner getting sick
As the Bridge Team goes ruffing along!
For it's a Hi, Hi, Hee!
We've got vulnerability!
Shout out "3 No Trump" loud and strong!
DOWN FOUR!
We will set the pace
As we trump our partner's ace —
And the Bridge Team goes ruffing along!

JOKE AND DAGGER DEPT. PART I

When Fidel (the man with the sword) ordered Antonio Prohias (the man with the pen) arrested for his anti-Castro cartoons, the Cuban artist fled to the U.S., where he now graces MAD's pages with . . .

133

134   END

PAGES FROM
A
SATIRIST'S
NOTEBOOK

BY HOWARD SCHNEIDER
WITH PICTURES BY *Clarke*

Once there was a man who was terribly unhappy because he was so short. His inferiority complex became so bad that he sought the help of a psychiatrist.

The good doctor managed to convince him that height was no obstacle, and that many short men had gone on to become millionaires. So now the man feels twice as bad as before because he's not only short... but poor!

There was once a family that was very unhappy because the

Momma and Poppa did not love each other and were only staying together for the sake of the children, and they were always fighting, and homelife was hell. So the children left home for the sake of the parents, who are still together, fighting, because now they have no one but each other.

137

Once there was a little boy who loved to sit in the bird bath in his parents' garden. No manner of persuasion could break him of this practice. And so, one quiet evening, his parents removed the bird bath from the garden. The next morning when the boy discovered what they'd done... he flew away!

138

The story is told of a young commercial artist who, after years of starving, suddenly became an overnight success.  His work was constantly in demand, and he commanded a fee of $30. an hour.

However, not being used to earning so much money, he soon discovered that a one-hour lunch cost him $30... a six hour nap cost him $180. ... and a ten-minute coffee break cost him exactly $5. So he gave them all up and worked himself to an early death ... but he left a huge estate!

END   139

In response to many requests (mostly from germs), the editors of MAD once again present a close-up look at that wonderful world-within-a-world . . . in

ANOTHER
MAD Peek
MICRO

Curious! It appears to be some
sort of invisible shield!!

Okay, Buster! Where's the heartburn!?

Through The
SCOPE

ARTIST: BOB CLARKE   WRITER: PHIL HAHN

To arms! To arms! The Miracle Drugs are coming!

Isn't that disgusting! One lousy bit part in a "Stripe" commercial...and he goes Hollywood on us!

The bacteria did it!

My problem is this recurring nightmare
in which I discover I'm not a germ at
all . . . just a psychosomatic illusion!

Then, Gentlemen, when you reach this point, a sneeze will automatically eject you, and you will be orbiting in outer space! Any questions?

Whattya say we all go down t'de Stomach ...an' start a rumble!?

Don Martin, MAD'S maddest artist, comes from a family of folk who draw. His brother draws flies, his sister draws blood, and his uncle draws unemployment insurance as . . .

THE HITCHIKER

THE EDITORS OF MAD

PRESENT

SOME VALENTINES WE SELDOM GET TO SEE

From a Housewife — to her Milkman

I've watched at dawn, while others sleep,
   How to my step you softly creep
And bring those goodies by the score
   To leave before my kitchen door.
Today, I plan that we should meet—
   (Me in my robe and cold bare feet;
You in your coat of dazzling white!)—
   To tell you of my heart's sad plight.
Yes, on this day of lovers, dear,
   I want to draw you very near
And whisper words just meant for you:
   "I'll take three quarts instead of two!"

149

From a Dentist — to his Lady Patient

My pressure leaps when I behold
Your fitted bridge, your crown of gold;
I find it hard to concentrate
When I adjust your lower plate;
Your caries set my heart on fire,
My poor head spins, my palms perspire.
You have a strange effect on me;
Oh, tell me, dear, what can it be?
Can it be love? No, that's not right!
It isn't love . . . it's *fear!* YOU BITE!

From A BARTENDER—
to his LADY CUSTOMER

PINK LADY - 75¢

PLASTERED LADY $1.00

Each day, when I unlock the bar,
  I know you'll soon be near
To crawl upon your favorite stool,
  And order gin and beer.
Your wish is my command, sweetheart;
  You get the very best
Imported wines and liquors, 'cause
  You are my favorite guest.
But there's a little secret
I think it's time you knew:
  And so, today, I'll whisper, "LUSH—
Your bar bill's *overdue!*"

From A Rich Old Man — To His Upstairs Maid

Fetch my robe and slippers, quick!
I think I am getting sick!
Stir the fire! I must nap!
Take my paper from my lap!
Turn the lamp down! Pull the shade!
Has my feather bed been made?
Brew some tea—three sugars, please!

Kleenex, quick! I'm going to sneeze!
Put the cat out! Lock the door!
Rub my neck a little more!
Rush and get my large pink pill!
I think I am getting ill!
Tuck me in, and dim the light!
One more thing, YOU'RE FIRED! Good night!

From A BOSS—
to his SECRETARY

Oh, lady of my heart's delight,
  Can you "work late" with me tonight?
First we will dine at some swank spot
  Where lights are low, and music's hot.
I need the proper atmosphere
  To make my proposition clear.
I have a lot I want to do,
    And, Hon, it all depends on you.
By the way, I thought I'd mention,
  So you'll know my true intention:
Tho you may think it's a crime,
  I plan to pay no over-time!

From A Mortician—to his Female Assistant!

SYMPATHY

Oh, lady of the rubber gloves
And antiseptic gown;
Of drainage tubes and bits of wire,
And pensive little frown;
Oh, lady of the steady hand
And nerves of tempered steel—
How can I ever tell you, Love,
Exactly how I feel?
We've been through much together, Sweet,
We've both worked side by side
Preparing all our clients for
That quiet, final ride,
It's nat'ral that I love you, Dear!
It's right that I should care!
You are the only girl I've seen
Without a glassy stare!

154   END

It is interesting to note that every comedian
approaches a subject in his own peculiar style.
Witness the rash of |astronaut| "bits" that have
been making the rounds recently—all different,
and all pretty funny. This uniqueness of style
and approach would still exist if, for example,
six comedians were to tell the very same joke!
To prove it, let's take a MAD look-listen at

six comics in search of a punchline

155

SHELLEY BERMAN

(PICKS UP PHONE, PUTS IT TO EAR, DIA
Hello? This is Doctor Schwartz! I'd like
to speak to Doctor Miller . . . **Schwartz!** Tha
capital S-C-H-W-A-R-T-Z . . . Oh, you kno
how to spell Schwartz! . . . **Doctor?** . . . Tha
capital D-O-C-T-O-R! You're welcome! . . . I
fine! . . . Fine! . . . Fine, thank you! Who am
talking to? . . . Oh, you're a **recording!** Tha
nice! . . . How **are** you? . . . oh, I'm fine! Fine
thank you! . . . No, there's no message! Jus
tell him I called to say 'Hello'! . . . **Hello!**
Capital H-E-L-L-O! . . . He's a psychiatrist
Let **him** figure it out!! (HANGS UP)

BO

156

HENNY YOUNGMAN

Two psychiatrists were
walking down a hall,
and one psychiatrist
said to the other—
"**Hello!**" And the other
psychiatrist said—
"Hmmm! I wonder what
he **meant** by that!"

EWHART

"sychiatry is a very big industry today!
ve—have you ever wondered what goes
. in the mind of one of those industrial-
ychiatrists at the end of a day? I'd—I'd
ike to **show** you what goes on in the
nind of—of one of those industrial—
•sychiatrists—at the end of—a day . . .
    (INTO CHARACTER)
Boy, I'm glad I'm rid of **those nuts!**
    Now to go home!
(DOOR OPENS AND CLOSES)
I'll—I'll just go down this corridor.
-oh! There's old Doctor Freen. He's—
e's also going home. I—um—er—I'd
etter say 'Hello' to old Doctor Freen.
-Why **should** I? Let **him** say 'Hello' to
e. N-no, he **wants** me to do that, so, he
feel **superior**. I-I **know** what I'll do.
-I'll confuse him completely. H-here
e comes . . . (LOUDLY) **Good-bye,**
ctor Freen! . . . (PAUSE) . . . Hmmm!
  I wonder what **I meant** by that?

BILL DANA
(AS JOSE JIMENEZ)

I would like to tell a hoke. A berry funny hoke. A hoke I once jeard tell by Jenny Youngman. It's a Jenny Youngman hoke— Two psychiatriss were walking down a jall an' one psychiatriss say to the other—"Jello!" An' the other psychiatriss, he say. "Jmmm! I wonder what **flabor?**"

MILTON BERLE

Two psychiatrists were walking down a hall, and one psychiatrist said to the other— **"Hello!"** And the other psychiatrist said— "Hmmm! I wonder what he **meant** by that!"

SAM LEVENSON

When I was a kid—*ha-ha*—remember?—*ha-ha!* Well, at that time Momma didn't know about psychiatry—*giggle-giggle!* But like all the mothers of her day, Momma was a psychiatrist in her own right—*ha-hah!* It's true! *Chortle-chortle!* Remember? Well, one day, Momma met another kid's Momma! And this Momma—*ha-hah!* said 'Hello' to my Momma. And my Momma didn't answer back. So—*chuckle-chuckle*—I asked Momma..."Momma, why didn't you answer 'Hello' when she said 'Hello'? *Ha-hah!* Now this is the beautiful part —and it's true—*giggle-giggle!* Momma said, "I didn't say 'Hello' to her 'Hello' because when she said her 'Hello', who knows what she meant?" *Giggle-guffaw-chortle-laugh—* —It's true!

BUMS AWAY DEPT.

In real life, if two unemployed clods roamed aimlessly around the country week after week, butting into people's lives, one of two things would happen to them. They'd either be arrested as vagrants or they'd be shot by citizens who value their privacy. But put these same two clods on TV, and what happens to them? They become heroes! You guessed it! We're talking about those two big heroes (and big bums) who appear on that weekly television series called

Route

Hold it! Hold it! **Cut! CUT!**

For cryin' out loud! Will you two guys get out from in front of our cameras! You're ruining our TV show! Where'd you guys come from, anyway? You're nothin' but a couple of **ugly bums!** The heroes in **OUR** show are a couple of **HANDSOME bums!**

And here come no Ready . Camera Action .

162

Excuse me, Madame! My handsome, illiterate friend and I are sort of wandering TV philosophers and psychologists. We ride up and down Route 67—except for a few 1,500 mile detours—helping miserable people solve their problems. Is there any little thing we can do for you—like finding a lost husband, solving financial problems, addressing the UN assembly?

Problems? I have no problems! I've got the kindest husband and the three most wonderful children in the world. Every once in a while, I get so overcome with happiness that I just break down like this . . . and cry for joy!

But surely, you must have SOME problems! Like a little insanity in the family, or the early stages of a disease! It doesn't have to be anything big!

G'wan! Get out of here, you trouble-makers! If you're not gone in one minute, I'll call the police!

163

Ladies and Gentlemen, tonight we have two noted visitors to Bayonne who are looking for people with problems. Now would you two bums— er—guys be good enough to tell our audience in what way you're both **qualified** for your jobs as **TV Problem-Solvers . . . ?**

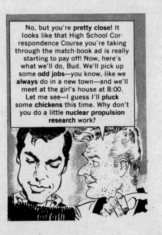

170

Now here's the way I see things in my meddlesome way! You were both **coddled** by your parents, so now you have this insatiable longing for **freedom**. And that's why you've become **traveling bums**. As for this obsession to **help other people**—well, it's really an unconscious desire to help **yourselves**. What I suggest is that you both get married and settle down in a cute **situation comedy** . . .

Now, I know two nice girls, Muriel and Bernice, who are **dying** to get married. They live right off Route 67 . . . about **1600 miles** right off it . . . over in the East Bronx. What you do is make a left turn at the next traffic light, and . . .

YOU
ARE
NOW
LEAVING
THE BRONX

THE CLAUS THAT DEPRESSES DEPT.

This is the season of the year when Crooners are dreaming of a "White Christmas"... and Store Owners are counting on a "Green" one! So before the Christmas Spirit passes out — with the arrival of the bills, MAD decks its pages with hunks of folly, and presents ...

172

A MAD LOOK AT

Christmas

When I was a boy, we used to bundle up warm, trudge through the snow, hike out into the woods, find a nice fir tree, chop it down, and haul it, for miles back to the house!

Today, they sell you a streamlined pile of metal consisting of a base, a pipe with holes, and some rods—which all fit together in 15 minutes—and they call THIS a Christmas Tree!!

I would like to order 500 of the most beautiful Christmas Cards you got!!

I want them to be deeply religious and solemn—with shepherds and the star and the three wise kings and the manger scene—you know—like that!

177

NUCLEAR JITTERS

Don Martin tells us why he quit the "Don Ameche Fan Club" . . .
mainly last time he used . . .

THE
TELEPHONE